*Touched
by God*

# Touched by God

A Collection of Prayers &
Reflections by
The Women's Community
Bible Study of Atlanta

Published by
Looking Glass Books
Dick Parker
219 Woodlawn Avenue
Decatur, Georgia    30030
(404) 371-1236

Manufactured in the United States of America
ISBN 0-9640852-3-2

# *ACKNOWLEDGMENTS*

There are always people that God uses to make a difference, to get the spark going, to see the potential and to encourage others toward a goal. The "spark" that inspired this undertaking was Pam Elting. She led others to organize and create this collection of prayers and reflections. All of these were lovingly written by the women of our Bible study, and many of them served as the opening prayer at our weekly meetings. We offer them here to bring glory to God and to provide a lasting tribute to our special friend, Marcia Hill.

We give thanks to God for using these women who were so dedicated to the development of *Touched by God* and its mission. They include: Story Evans and Mary Inman, who tirelessly typed the entire manuscript, plus Lane Irby, Indy Cesari, Marianne Craft, Gwynie Dennard, Linda Elliot, Kathy Lee, Nell Long, Nancy McGuirk, Candy Morgan, Jeannie Ross, Treacy Shaw, Susan Welsh, Linda Wyatt and Margaret Young.

We also give thanks for the many people who prayed for God's hand to guide each page.

We are grateful to the many members of WCBS who so generously made financial contributions to this project.

# *FOREWORD*

*A*nytime I read the Bible I am continually amazed at how God touches one life after another, changes their course midstream, and brings them into a greater understanding of who He is! The result, for those who respond, is always a grateful heart and a life full of love, meaning and purpose.

"Does God still touch people today?" we ask. ABSOLUTELY! And He touches each person in a different way. We mistakenly look for, even long for, that burning bush experience of Moses or the blinding light of Paul. Yet while there are still exceptions today (for we would never limit God), for the most part God comes to us in the quietness of our lives. As the Lord said, "Be still and know that I am God." Or, as Elijah discovered, God was not in the storm but in the whisper of life.

Can we hear Him or recognize His presence in our life if we are not still? For if we are not focused on Him, we are focused on something else. How can we know God better? I have often thought that if Moses or Paul were alive today, they would remind us that we have something that they did not have, God's written Word, the Bible. God speaks to us through His Word by telling us who He is and by giving us advice on how to live our lives. We so often turn to self-help books, psychologists, or counselors for help...only to realize that the best source for help is probably collecting dust on our shelf. As we spend time in prayer and studying God's Word, we come to know Him better and experience Him at work in our lives. And the more you know Him, the more you love Him.

This book is about a group of women who have been touched by God. They began as a small group of believers who came together to study God's Word to know Him better. For two years they met weekly for prayer time and Bible study. These two years were not without tragedies. Two of the women lost children, one lost her husband, two went through financial difficulties, and two were transferred from the city. Through all this, they came to know and love God. They learned that God is to be trusted for who He is and not what He does or allows to happen in our lives. As their faith was stretched, so was their character, and they began to look beyond themselves. The door was opened to the community, and today over 250 women heard the call and fill a chapel weekly for worship, prayer and fellowship in what has come to be known as the Women's Community Bible Study.

As different as all of these women are, equally different is the way in which God has touched their lives, and the lives of their families. All in all, they share one common thread...a grateful heart and a desire to express it. These prayers and reflections are offered for the glory of God and bring a very simple message...that God is still very much at work today! May you too be touched by His power and love!

*Nancy McGuirk*

## TO MARCIA HILL

The Scriptures tell us, "Those who hope in the Lord will renew their strength. They will soar on wings like eagles, they will run and not grow weary, they will walk and not be faint." Many people witnessed Marcia Hill live this Scripture. She was given wings of strength, courage and grace and a beautiful radiance to meet each day. For you see, Marcia was touched by God; her hope and her faith were in Him.

Five years ago, Marcia, a pretty, talented wife, mother of four, successful business woman, and friend to many, was diagnosed with cancer. Many walked her battle with her as she fought for her life; and in turn she taught us all how to live. She came to our Bible Study to know God and to study His Word. As she began to surrender her life to Him, her life was never the same. Christ made His home in her heart, and in her weakness she was made strong. She taught us all that life was a precious gift—that we must love a lot, forgive a lot, and slow down. She enabled us to believe in our capacity as human beings when we partner our lives with God. She gained a new perspective: Christ's eyes to see, His heart to love unconditionally, and His power to triumph over obstacles and pain. As many shared in her struggle and her hope for a miracle of physical healing, we were all very aware of the daily miracles that were taking place in her life in so many ways. She came to our Bible Study to be ministered to and ended up ministering to everyone else.

God used Marcia to touch all of us and we are forever grateful to have known her and to have been God's witnesses to the miracle of her life. This book is dedicated to her loving memory.

*Touched
by God*

# GOD'S GRACE, MY GRACE

*W*hen I was sixteen my family experienced two tragedies. Both were life changing for me. I remember my father sitting me down and explaining something to me that I shall never forget. He said, "We all have a cross to bear in our lifetime. Each individual has his or her own. It will be something so difficult and heavy that unless we have a true faith we will not be able to withstand it. It will be God's grace that will sustain us—if only we lean on Him." My Dad went on to say that these two tragedies were not my cross—I would have one of my own sometime in my lifetime.

On the morning of Dec. 24, 1991, nineteen years later, I realized what my father had been trying to tell me.

It was a chilly Christmas Eve morning and I arrived at the hospital to deliver my third child. I "knew" everything would be fine because I had been seen by my doctor just fifteen hours earlier and he said, "The heart beat is as steady as a drum." But in the pre-op room, (a c-section was to be done), they told me that my infant son's heart had stopped. "I am so very sorry," was all the nurses could say.

From that moment on I felt like I was in an airtight elevator descending rapidly downward. I could hear kind voices in the distance but I couldn't really focus on what they were saying. I just kept descending lower, lower and lower.

This was Christmas Eve—everyone was preparing for one of the happiest days of the year. It was a time to sing Christmas carols, light candles at church, and hang stockings—not plan a funeral.

All I could think was that this couldn't be real and it couldn't be happening to me. God was good and my Lord would not take my child from me, especially on Christmas Eve. Not my SAVIOR.

The elevator I spoke of finally hit rock bottom.

I began to get angry. I knew I wasn't always good, but I couldn't imagine having done something so awful to caused me this much pain and the shattering of my heart and faith.

This was my cross to bear and in bearing it I learned the true meaning of SAVIOR. I learned of a deeply personal relationship that not only involved my night time prayers but an open line of communication 24 hours of the day with Christ.

I learned that Christ did not cause me to lose my son, but "life" and being human did. He never turned his back on me even though I turned away from Him. He patiently waited for me, sending love my way in thoughts, words and deeds. Prayers, friends, letters, listeners, helpers came my way just when I needed them the most.

When I finally quit blaming Him, he carried me through the most difficult time of my life. I had to allow Him to do this for me. He does not force his way into our lives; He comes upon invitation. When I couldn't sleep, he comforted me. When I couldn't communicate, He waited patiently. When I had to do all the things that a mother of two wonderful elementary school children had to do, He gave me the strength.

We had a relationship before the death of my son but now we have a personal ongoing dialog with one another, and I can't imagine trying to do anything again on my own.

He has given me my life and He has carried my cross with me.

On May 4, 1995, God blessed me with my fourth child. Her name is Grace.

"I am convinced that neither death nor life, nor angels nor principalities, nor things to come, nor powers, nor height nor depth, nor anything else in all creation, will be able to separate me from the love of God that is in Christ Jesus my Lord. ( Romans 8:38-39)

"You have blessed me and Kept me; You have made Your face shine upon me and have been gracious to me; You have turned Your face toward me and given me peace." (Numbers 6:24-26)

*Gwynie Dennard*

## THE DIVINE SPARK

*H*elp us, Lord, please,
   To love You and to love one another.
   Please, Holy God,
   Add to each of us a "Divine Spark,"
   That our Lights may shine with more joy, hope,
peace, wisdom, patience, trust and love.
   Please help us and bless us with Your strength to
obey as Jesus.
   Let us shine with Your love, Lord,
   Let us wait with Your patience.
   Let us feel Your peace and smile with Your joy.
   Let us go forth in Your wisdom and guidance.
   Let us love with Your love.
   Thank you for Your many blessings.
   We ask in Christ's name.
   Amen

   *Lane Irby*

## ON THAT ROAD

Lord, I am on that road to Damascus,
With a past that has hold of me.
I have been blinded by my transgressions,
Will You open my eyes to see?

I am filled with my own accomplishments,
Pride and possessions to name a few
But none of these will matter, Lord
When I open my eyes to You.

Am I worthy of Your message,
Lord? I wonder as I walk
Along that hot, dry road to Damascus
The growing evil in me stalks.

My mind and heart cannot be opened
Until the Holy Spirit draws near
And redirects the walk I'm taking
And, by grace, my Lord appears.

The blinding past I put behind me
And, through faith, I now can see
The chains that bound me on my walk
He has broken...and set me free.

*Kathy Lee*

# *DRAWING NEAR TO GOD*

*T*here are two times a year that challenge my walk with God more so than ever — May and December. Too often, I let the world, its demands, its "busyness," rob me of the fullness that is mine in Christ. I tend to make bad choices about how to prioritize at the most challenging times of the year for me. As a result, I find myself out of touch with God and myself, and I am left feeling alone, detached, fragmented, and ineffective. I have come to know that we are ultimately as intimate with God as we ourselves choose to be. We live on the stormy, broken surface of life. Christ calls us to himself; it is our choice to respond. For it is in Him that we find our rest, our balance, our power, and our fulfillment. To Him, I can relinquish my burdens, my agenda, my struggles, my limited viewpoints, and the momentum of my life. And in Him, I can be replenished, restored, and energized anew.

So if in my lifetime I am to know God intimately, His will for me, and His peace, then I must discipline myself to abide in Christ daily. In the midst of the noise and the pull of our world, how do I quiet myself in order to become sensitive to God's indwelling spirit. I must first find my meeting place with God. Whenever I feel Him most intimately, I need to go there daily for reflective prayer, meditation, and the reading of His Word. A daily morning appointment needs to go on my calendar. Otherwise, something else will clamor for my attention. When I close out the world for a small part of my day, all of life becomes spiritual as my heart is focused on Him. When I allow Christ to make His home in my heart, I am given greater capacity as a human being. For it is in this life of surrender and trust that I give up my right to be in control and I experience the fullness and the freedom of a spirit-filled life. My desire is that I be molded by You, Lord, and not by the world. Use me as Your servant so I might glorify You in all things.

Thank You, Lord, that You allowed me to experience a life apart from You in order that I might know my need for You always. Draw me to a place of solitude daily, and enable me to quiet myself and to abide in You. Give me Your eyes to see and to understand. Give me Your heart to love unconditionally, and your power to triumph over obstacles and pain. Amen

*Pam Elting*

## DIVERGING PATHS

*D*ear Heavenly Father,
     As we face each new dawn, we are offered diverging paths upon which to trod. One leads to a partnership with the world and its fleeting prizes. The other leads to immeasurable joy, peace and eternal communion with You in Your Heavenly Kingdom. Each road beckons as we start a new day with promises for our fulfillment.

The world offers to open doors that we may achieve better opportunities. You open windows so that we may soar in the assurance of Your love and grace. The world praises us for self-accomplishment and acknowledges the best that we are. You recognize our selfless accomplishments and see in us the best that we might become. The world keeps us down and You, Lord, lift us up. The world promises shortcuts for many of life's travels. You teach us that there are no short cuts but the trip is well worth taking. The world teaches us how to put out fires as we race through our daily lives. You teach us how to start fires in the hearts and souls of those around us for the love of Jesus Christ. The world loves us because of who we are. You love us in spite of who we are.

The one road is clearly mapped with worldly rewards at each destination. The other road has no map at all. We ask for Your strength as we choose our daily pathway. Give us discernment, clear minds and hearts, and the ability to keep our eyes focused on You. Help us turn away from the path of the world with its illusion of grandeur, and direct us toward Your path with its inclusion in the grandeur of Your Heavenly Kingdom. This we pray, in Jesus' precious name. Amen

*Susan King*

## HERE I AM

*T*hen you shall call, and the Lord will answer; You shall cry for help, and He will say 'Here I Am.' "
Isaiah 58:9

Our Dear Heavenly Father,

We come to You each day, each hour, with great humility. We need You and ask for Your help, Your wisdom, Your power and Your strength as we confess our sins to You. We ask not only for Your forgiveness, but also for Your insights into our wrongdoings. While trying to be more Christlike, forgive us when we continue our human misbehavior.

Thank You, Father, for Your loving, ever-caring Holy Spirit who is our guide and helper. You know our every thought and deed even before we speak or act. In happiness, crisis, or sadness You are always available for us. When we cry to You, You say, "Hear I Am," providing comfort for our hearts. Thank You for Your perfect love and wisdom for our lives. When we cry to You in terrible pain and distress, You are our comforter. If we relinquish our control to You, You show us Your wonderful peace, even in the midst of unbearable pain.

Lord, we have so much to learn in our walk on this earth. Help us to take each step holding Your hand and relying on Your guidance for us. We want to walk beside You, not ahead or behind. Then, we can renew our strength and mount up with wings like eagles. We want to run and not be weary, walk and not faint.

Thank You, Lord, for Your perfect and powerful plan for our lives and for Your world. In Jesus Name, Amen

*Ree Hoffman*

## GRACE IN ADVERSITY

*B*lessed is the man who trusts in the Lord and whose trust is the Lord. For he will be like a tree planted by the water, that extends its roots by a stream."
Jeremiah 17:7, 8

Trees of all shapes and sizes have always captured my eye and my heart, so the magnificent wild magnolia tree growing for years in my front yard is very dear to me. I have watched it bloom with its lush white blossoms and flourish with huge green leaves and have been amazed by its beauty.

During a construction project recently, one large limb about twenty feet off the ground was broken and left dangling out of reach. So it hung there all winter and grieved me. I took some comfort in knowing it would eventually fall off and the rest of the tree would continue to prosper.

Spring has finally returned, and this morning as I sat on the front porch taking in the beauty of new growth all around, I was shocked to see green leaves and white blossoms on the end of my pitiful "dead" limb. It struck me that the limb, though clearly broken, had to have some connection to the life-giving trunk and roots. The sweet and sad truth hit me that the limb was enabled to give 'its best' even though broken and certainly dying. I thought of the powerful truth that His strength is perfected in our weakness (2 Cor. 12:10). I also thanked the Lord for the touching image he gave me from my beloved tree of His certain and unending source of strength and enabling in my life as I abide in Him.

How often I feel like that broken limb, struggling in my faith. We all have seen others suffer great sorrow and injustices and even death and yet the grace and life of the Lord is so evident in them. The rest of the verse from Jeremiah 17: 7,8 brings our true hope into focus..."Blessed is the man who trusts in the Lord...for he will be like a tree planted by the water, that extends its roots by a stream and will not fear when the heat comes; but its leaves will be green, and it will not be anxious in a year of drought nor cease to yield fruit." Amen

*Sandy Browning*

## USE ME

ear Lord,
   Use me.

Use me as an extension of Your love so that others may feel Your presence.

Use me to accomplish the work that needs to be completed so that others will know that God never leaves a job unfinished.

Use me to be that listening ear to someone in pain so that others will know of Your gentleness.

Use me to see what others cannot see so that they will know of Your empathy.

Use me to walk a troubled road so that others may learn of Your faithfulness.

Use me to carry heavy burdens so that others will understand Your steadfastness.

Use me as a good mother so that children may grow up to know You as their personal Savior.

Use me to be a better wife so that my husband will understand Your unconditional love.

Use me to be a better friend so that others will know of Your compassion.

Use me, Lord, for Your sake, under any circumstance, for as long as it takes in order for others to experience You more personally.

Until we meet in paradise,
Gwynie

*Gwynie Dennard*

## GRACE IN THE DEEPEST OF SORROWS

*F*ive years ago today, our little girl, Carey, died. I almost allowed the heaviness of my sorrow to bury me along with her. I allowed the anger and bitterness that raged in my soul to radically change my relationship with God. I did not speak to Him for months and when I did, it was always in a blasphemous and venomous manner.

In the sorrow-filled months that followed, I came to know and understand several things about God that had only been empty words before. I came to a new understanding of trust. Before, I had not truly trusted in the character of God. I had trusted in His ability to do and be what I wanted Him to do and be.

I came to know the true meaning of unconditional love. In spite of my actions and my harsh words, He continued to surround me with people to love me and care for me and nurture me. That was how He embraced me lovingly.

I came to a new understanding of how God works in His "mysterious ways." When I felt I could not take another baby step forward, a note of encouragement would be in the mailbox or left on the porch with a bunch of handpicked flowers; the message machine would be loaded with simple prayers and empathy from total strangers who too had lost a child; Father Purcell's, the Godly home for terminally ill children, that had heard our story, suddenly had room for Carey; a hug from someone in the grocery store. I know that God uniquely and timely placed each of these loving acts of kindness squarely in front of me and my family to move us one step closer to healing.

I came to know Grace in its finest hour. Grace—that infusion of blessing and strength when you least expect it and when you least deserve it. The treasures I have watched born out of this very dark and tragic time—Carey's Foundation that helps breathe life into the living after loss of child, the House Next Door, the deeper, compassionate side of our children who also lost, and, finally, a husband and father whose relationship with God blossomed and grew into its own little ministry. The prayer here was taken from my "grief journal" that I continue to write as the healing process with God's help continues. Following it is a prayer written by my daughter, Mary Radford.

*D*earest Father in Heaven,
  My heart is so heavy with grief, I can hardly find the strength to get to my knees to pray. The only words that come to me at the moment are not even my own. They are the words of David in Psalm 31, "Be gracious to me, O Lord, for I am in distress, my eye is wasted from grief, my body and soul also, my eyes are red from weeping, my health is broken from sorrow." Please, Lord, I awoke today with a newness of spirit, a sense of joy, a desire to live and to live life abundantly. I am beginning to understand Your Divine Gift—Grace— thank You for showering me with it. Today the scripture Isaiah 40:29 came to life for me like manna from Heaven. " He gives power to the tired and worn out, and strength to the weak. They that wait upon the Lord shall renew their strength." Thanks be to God. Amen

*Linda Wyatt*

$\mathcal{D}$ear Lord,
Please bless Marcia Hill's family. Help them to
know what a great place she is in. Please tell Marcia to
find my baby sister and hold her and let them play
together.

*Mary Radford Wyatt*
*Age 10*
*Daughter of Linda Wyatt*

# A CHRISTMAS PRAYER

*T*hank you Lord for the many gifts we receive daily.

Thank you so much for our cherished lives. Please help us to realize that just because we were given life does not mean that we do not need to give something in return. Thank you for each breath that we take, for each very special leaf that blows softly in the wind and for the miracle of life. Thank you for this special time that we are able to quiet our hearts, be with our beloved families, and to give thanks for all of our many blessings.

**Christ**, the Son of our Heavenly Father was born in a filthy stable. He was such a small and helpless infant. In his tiny hands He held the future of all people.

**H**atred never filled His heart yet he died on the cross brutally so our sins would be forgiven for all evil taking place.

**R**ise up from all evil and find grace in the Lord.

**I** alone am helpless but help is found in the Lord.

**S**uch a small child He was yet there is no measure for His greatness.

The wonders of our Lord are numerous, so let us explore all of the gifts that our Lord has to offer.

May we remember at this wonderful time how lucky and fortunate we are to have such a loving and caring God.

As we travel the roads of our lives, let us remember to stay with our Lord and praise him the whole way for all that has been given to us.

Seek love and knowledge from the Lord and you will always be surrounded by his love.

*Emily Hill*
*Age 13*
*Daughter of Marcia Hill*

# A PRAYER OF DISCOVERY AND THANKS

*D*ear Lord,
    I have been away from You and Your love for so long. I praise You for taking me back in Your loving arms. On January 30, 1996, at a women's Bible study seminar conducted by a Christian speaker, I recommitted my life to Jesus Christ. Life is joyous again.

My best friend, my mother, died from cancer twenty years ago. Her life was cut short, and as a young college student, I was bitter and angry. I blamed You, God. Now, after studying Your Word weekly in Bible study, I realize that You had a plan for her life. I was too selfish to see that. Please forgive me, O Lord.

Now, I can see that You have a plan for my life too. It is only now that I can look back and see all the wonderful ways You have been working in my life. You have blessed me with good health, a loving husband and two beautiful children. You have shown me a way to work out of my home so that I can be a full-time mother. Oh, how I praise You and thank You for these precious blessings.

Thank you, Lord, for leading me to a special friend who introduced me to a Bible study group. The number of new Christian friends I have found there is awesome. I am eager to get to know each and every one of these precious women better. And, most importantly, Lord, You have led me back to Your Son, Jesus Christ. Help me walk the walk daily and to follow the teachings of Jesus.

Thank you, Lord, for introducing me to Christian authors who have led me to discover the awesome power of daily prayer. I believe, Lord, that Your personal plan for my life will affect the world around me. Help me to commit to spend time with You daily in prayer.

Also, dear Lord, help me continue to spend time with You, diligently looking for You and listening to You through Your Word and Spirit. Specifically, help me to continue to increase and build my faith and to spread Your Word and Jesus' teachings to others.

Most of all, Lord, help me to develop a personal, loving relationship with You and an incredible love for You.

I ask these things in Jesus Christ's name. Amen.

*Phoebe Boychuk*

# HEALING FROM THE INSIDE OUT (GOD'S WAY!)

*A* friend and I had lunch together some time ago. She was a nurse and was working with a patient whose wound had healed at the surface rather than from the inside. The result was an open wound underneath causing extensive infection. She explained that the doctor must then cut the skin again, and use stainless steel prongs to hold the wound open so it would heal properly—from the inside out.

As she explained the healing process, I reflected upon my own circumstances and the crushing pain I was experiencing at the time. Was this an illustration from God for me; was I like the patient in my friend's story? Had I covered up my pain only to have it become infected underneath? And was I willing to take the time and effort to allow God to heal me properly—from inside? I wondered if my avoidance of the pain prolonged my spiritual healing.

Pain is often the purifying element that allows others to see Christ in us. It purifies our motives and refines our character. Although usually unpleasant, when we allow God to heal us His way, we are healed from the inside out.

"We can rejoice too, when we run into problems and trials for we know that they are good, for us—they help us learn to be patient. And patience develops strength of character in us and helps us trust God more each time we use it, until finally our hope and faith are strong and steady. Then, when it happens, we are able to hold our heads high no matter what happens and know that all is well, for we know how dearly God loves us. We feel this warm love everywhere within us because God has given us the Holy Spirit to fill our hearts with his love." Romans 5:3-5, The Living Bible.

*Anne Irwin*

# A GRATEFUL HEART OVERFLOWING

*D*ear Heavenly Father,
It is 6:30 a.m. on Saturday and I cannot sleep. I am filled with gratitude, appreciation, love and praise.

Yesterday, as I drove my oldest child to school, we started to pray (she always reminds me to keep my eyes open as I drive). I clenched her hand and spoke to you, "Lord, please help my daughter sing for you glory." (She was singing two solos for her school concert.)

Lord, as I later sat and watched her and listened to her beautiful voice, I was totally filled with your love and joy. You have given me so many blessings, but the greatest blessing I felt at the moment I heard her sing was the incredible love I have for my family. My daughter stood up then, all grown up — no footie pajamas, no braces, no curls — a beautiful young Christian woman. I realized how little time we have on this earth to love, give to, and nurture the ones we care for.

Dear Father, please keep me focused on the "real" things in life — relationships with my family and friends. Help me always to rejoice in the small blessings of yesterday and today.

I praise Your name for your gifts to me — my

husband, my children, my extended family and my precious friendships. I thank you for giving me a part of You that helps me to love and reach out to others.

Father, please make me a better wife, mom, daughter, sister, and friend — only to glorify Your name, and let my life be a reflection of who You are.

My gift to You this morning is my grateful heart overflowing. I am completely in awe of Your sweet blessings in my life. Words cannot express the feelings I have of being one of those chosen to know You in this way. We all have the opportunity, and I thank You for allowing me to "hang on."

You can only know in my heart, and not in these words, how truly grateful I am for You and Your love for me.

I love you now and forever.

*Cindy Hewlett*

# HE EMBRACES OUR FAMILIES

*W*hat does being part of a family mean?

Birthday, laughter, ball games, celebrations, sleep overs, camp outs, impromptu ice cream, skinny dippin' in the summer, first dates, vacations, friends, graduation, Mother's Day, Father's Day, back rubs, bedtime stories and unconditional love.

It also means disappointments, strained relationships, misunderstandings, discipline, tears, unkind words, broken promises, regrets, failures, alienation, discontentment, depression, heartache, sickness and death.

It has been through my most painful family circumstances that I have experienced my closeness with God and an absolute knowledge that He is in control and has a hopeful future for each and every one of us. It is my prayer that as moms and dads we will claim God's promise in Jeremiah 29:11 that says: "For I know the plans I have for you, and I will bless you with a future filled with hope, a future of success, not of suffering." I pray that no matter what Satan throws our family's way, God will be that Rock, that Mighty Fortress; our Protector; our Encourager; our Strength; that we might be more Christlike as parents, and therefore, pass on that baton, which is a gift and a blessing Satan cannot touch. Amen

*Terry Henritze*

# IN THANKSGIVING FOR MOTHERS

*D*ear Precious Father,
Thank you for the mothers in our lives. They were the vessel through which You entered our world. They gave us our first angel's kiss as we emerged, they held us gently in their arms and bathed our first sunlight with warmth and joy.

You could have come on stallions with gold chariots and flashing lights, and yet You chose a quiet beginning with a mother in a manger in a stable. That very night You blessed us with the privilege that Mary has passed down to all generations: to be the first to hold and to touch, to give new life and to nurture.

Mothers give us an opportunity to feel God's unselfish and sacrificial love. They allow us to see more clearly the unique relationship they share with Christ:

For as mothers gave us birth...Jesus gives us life.

As mothers raise according to principles...Jesus knew we could never live up to all of them.

As mothers love us unconditionally...Jesus stretched out His arms on the cross, and gave His life for us.

Thank you, God, for the mothers in our lives. Just

as you chose Mary for Your own Son, so You have chosen mothers for each of us. When being a mother means giving more than we receive, when this anointed office seems more of a struggle than a joy and more of a burden than a blessing, help us to remember that we were called and blessed and given access always to Your love and support.

And when mothering means letting go, give us the strength to trust in You and release.

Thanks be to God.

*Kathy Lee*

# *OPEN OUR HEARTS*

*L*et us Pray—
Our Father who art in heaven
Hallowed be Thy name
Thy kingdom come
Thy will be done
On earth as it is in heaven
Give us this day our daily bread
And forgive us our trespasses
As we forgive those who trespass against us
And lead us not into temptation
But deliver us from evil
For Thine is the kingdom, and the power and the glory. Forever. Amen

Lord, bring Your light to every single soul who reads this prayer to open their heart's eyes to see You in everything and receive Your presence.

Lord, the words of the Holy Scripture of the Old Testament are still so very true and pertinent today.

Bless us to know You, love You, trust You, and obey You. If, in Your mercy, Your people turn back to You, bless their worship and praise with total rebuke of cancer, rebuke of all ills in our world.

    Bring us back toward the garden.

    Worthy is the Lamb in whose name we pray.

Amen

*Lane Irby*

# INTIMACY WITH OUR SAVIOUR

*M*ost Gracious Heavenly Father,
Thank you for the privilege of coming before
You in the name of Jesus with our prayers this day and
every day. Thank You that You hear our prayers and
long to graciously bestow Your blessings and mercies on
all who are called in accordance with Your will. We are
truly a fellowship of believers bound by the Holy Spirit
as one in Christ. Heavenly Father, You have so blessed
us through this fellowship, having revealed to each one
the path to intimacy with our Savior, the only source of
true peace and joy. May it be our utmost desire to seek
that intimacy with all our hearts, and may we begin on
our knees humbling ourselves and seeking Your face.
Forgive us for the inevitable times when we are fearful
to look within and face the necessary changes. For You
showed us, Lord, that even as we professed You as Lord
and Savior with our mouths, our hearts still belonged to
the world.  At the same time, Father, You are gentle
enough to receive us where we are, nudging and encouraging our trust through the Holy Spirit, molding us to
be all You have called us to be.

Lord, we are renewed and recharged by the power

of Your Holy Spirit. Our light shines and we thank You that others have seen it, that You may be glorified. For we have experienced true fellowship with the Living God and the joy that comes with it. This is Your gift to us and may we desire it every day above all else. Bless us, Lord, and fill us with Your wisdom and strength. May we submit to Your Holy Spirit as our teacher and guide. Grant us ears to hear, eyes to see and a desire to serve. May we long to be women after Your own heart and seek to make a difference in our hearts and homes for You.

In Christ's name we pray. Amen

*Sharon Wilson*

## GIVE US TRUSTING SPIRITS

*D*ear Father,
Help! You have created a world of music, laugh-ter, joy and breathtaking beauty. How do we absorb such wonder amidst our increasing knowledge of pain and strife that infiltrates every area of Your magnificent creation?

I pray that You enable us as individuals, families and communities to be responsible for all that You've given us and, as we reach out to those in need, that You protect our struggling spirits. I pray that You grace us with discernment so that we may recognize when the greater need is within our own families. We sometimes overlook those closest to us because it requires such energy to resolve conflict and confront issues with our loved ones. Oftentimes, the affirmation that we receive outside of our families is unavailable from within. This is when we must rely on Your guidance and trust in Your goodness. Please give us trusting spirits!

You have blessed us with extraordinary abun-dance. Keep us strong in Your Word and humble servants as we seek to follow Your Son's greatest commandment, "Love the Lord your God with all your heart, with all your soul and with all your mind." (Matthew 22:37,38)

*Marianne K. Craft*

# A PRAYER FOR THE CHURCH: PALM SUNDAY

*D*ear Lord,
   On this cloudy day we yearn for the coming beauty of spring, while we remember another spring day two millennia ago when Your Son entered Jerusalem triumphant...

   We reflect on the coming week of betrayal, and on the redeeming power of the Cross, and on the Resurrection...

   We wanted a king and You gave us a Savior...

   We remember among us those who are in sickness, that you would bring them healing...

   We remember among us those who are in separation, that you would bring them to their loved ones...

   We remember among us those who are grieving, that you would bring them comfort...

   We remember among us those who are confused and hurting in a changing world of insecurity and job transition. Comfort them in the sure knowledge that in this difficult time You have wonderful plans for them also...

   Give us Your direction for reaching out to penetrate our pagan culture, to deliver the redemption of Your Gospel.

Show us the way to reach our older people, rich in experience but seeking meaning in their lives...

Show us the way to reach our single mothers and fathers, struggling to raise their children by themselves in a secular world without values...

Show us the way to reach our college and graduate students so rich in youth and enthusiasm for Your Word. Encourage their fervor...

Show us the way to reach our widows and widowers, approaching life with an unaccustomed loneliness...

Show us the way to reach the poor and homeless in this rich land, who need not just food and shelter, but the renewing spirit of the Gospel of Jesus Christ, to know that they too are loved...

Help us to give to all of Your people the good news and salvation of Your Gospel, and to do our part to bring Your Kingdom to this earth. As we serve others help each of us Lord to be stepping stones and not stumbling blocks for Your purpose, so that our church will in all things glorify Your Holy Name.

In Jesus' name we pray... Amen

*Carolyn McClatchey*

# *HE SINGS OVER US WITH JOY*

*F*ather,
Thank You that we belong to You and You are always calling us to Yourself. I marvel at how much You love us. You knew we would try to go our own way but still You made us in Your image and long for us to come into Your Presence. You sing over us with joy and call us Your Beloved.

Please help us today to be quiet and peaceful enough to listen for Your still small voice. Forgive us when we do not come to You early to hear Your voice and Your plan for our day. I want to know You more. I want to walk with You every moment of every day. Soften my heart that I would feel Your compassion for those You place in my path today. O gracious Father, how blessed we are to be called children of the living God. Help us to truly trust You and give You praise for all things. Keep us ever close to Your heart that Your love can flow through us to this lost and dying world.

I love You, Lord, and wait upon You. Cover us with Your protection and show us the Way.

In Jesus' Matchless Name, Amen

*Paula Smith*

# *HIS BLESSINGS ABOUND*

*A*lmighty God,
What a joy it is to have fellowship with one another! Thank You for these women who are gathered here today. Father, we come from so many different backgrounds. Even as recently as this morning, our lives have taken us in many directions—from pre-school carpools to professional careers to maybe just a quiet morning alone. We are as varied as our number. Yet, we have gathered here to have fellowship with one another, desiring each other's company, coming together as one united group of friends.

Thank You for blessing each of us with this caring and supportive neighborhood. Thank You for each person who has served so willingly this year, giving of their time and heart to reach beyond themselves to bless others. Show us daily how we can truly love our neighbor—a kind word, a helping hand or a listening ear.

We pray that You will slow us down, for we know that we live too fast. With all eternity before us, make us take time to live, time to get acquainted with Thee, time to enjoy Your blessings, and time to know each other. Amen

*Marcia Gaddis*

# INSPIRED BY A "SIMPLE CARPENTER"

*D*ear Father,
Thank You for the gift of life and for Your Holy Spirit. You have inspired us as we gathered together as a group to hear and study Your Word and to grow in Your knowledge and grace.

Help us to keep in mind that our religion began with a group of people following a man down a dusty road. These people were fishermen, Lord, not easily deceived.

Though understanding theological doctrines and remembering scripture are both important to our Christian growth, we have learned that it is essential that we are drawn to His humanness. That we come to know that Nazarene carpenter so that we can honestly ask ourselves that question: "Do I want to be changed into His likeness?"

And so we began our journey together, women studying, sharing, praying together. We found Christ in our sufferings and our joys. We welcomed new life, we mourned the loss of loved ones, we began to feel the blessings of a Christ-centered community, for when we felt separated from Christ, He was there in that same community to bring us back, to take our brokenness and restore us, to give back a whole person infused with Christ. We never left as the same person.

Our Christ, our God, our Child began to grow from an image to a real person. A friend inviting us to know Him and join Him in His work. A physician who promises to heal when there is no cure. A father in whose arms we can be embraced. A son who walks among us and gives His life for us yet asks only in return that we love. And a spirit who moved and breathed from the beginning of time and who moves in each of us today. God is alive and in touch with every aspect of our lives. If the life of Marcia Porter Hill taught us anything it was that joy was not the absence of suffering but the presence of God.

As we gathered together each week we left for those few moments our noisy and active world, our demands, our own desires, to learn about this man called Jesus. Many of us gave our life to Him and all of us began our own personal journeys to be changed into his likeness. Thanks be to God.

*Kathy Lee*

# A JOURNEY CONTINUING

*A*lmost six years ago my life was changed forever because of the relationship I was to have with thirteen women. God touched our hearts and minds and with the Holy Spirit leading us, we began a journey that continues on. The Women's Community Bible Study molded me and awakened a realization that I needed God in my life. I learned that through daily prayer, Bible study and an open heart, a deeper relationship with God would evolve. It was extremely difficult when I had to move and leave these very special friends, but I knew in my heart that this was God's plan for my family. We've been in Dallas for three years and, as my faith has grown, my heart is filled with love and gratitude for these friends and their prayers for my family. I thank God that I was a part of such a special group.

As I get older and continue to learn God's Word, I realize that teaching His Word to our children is the most important challenge we have as parents. This is a prayer I pray daily.

Dear Heavenly Father,
I thank You for the most wonderful gifts in the

world, my children. They are such blessings to us and I thank You for their health, their minds and their wonderful, sweet personalities. God, please give me the wisdom, patience and energy to be a good parent. Please wrap Your arms around them and protect them from evil. Please mold them into loving, caring people. Please open their hearts and minds so that they will know You and love You, for if they have You in their hearts, everything in life falls into place. In Jesus name I pray.

Amen

*Ann Gernert*

# LIFE IN YOUR RESURRECTED POWER

*L*ord, Please help us to live in Your Resurrection Power.

Let the Light of Your Divine Love — The Great I Am — bless us to *receive* from You.

And then, Lord, bless us to *overflow* in Your will, in obedience to You alone.

We humbly beseech You to shine through us, Your vessels.

Please fill us up to overflow as we abide in You.

We pray in Your name.  Amen

*Anonymous*

# *WE CAN WALK IN HIS LIGHT*

*D*ear Heavenly Father,
   We praise Your Holy Name. We are in awe of Your mighty power, love, mercy and grace.

   Forgive us if we have overlooked our brother or sister in need—in our own families and neighborhoods, as well as in families and neighborhoods that are less fortunate.

   Enable us to do Your will. Please give us the strength to endure Your discipline. Let us know that You have called us daughters, that You will never take anything away without replacing it with something better. You will turn our tragedies to triumphs, our poverty to riches, our pain to glory, and our defeat to victory. You have set Your seal of ownership on us and put Your spirit in our hearts as a deposit, guaranteeing what is to come—that You raised the Lord from the dead, and that You will raise us also.

   Thank You, thank You, thank You that You have searched for us and that You have interceded for us and that we can walk in the Light of Jesus Christ and His hope and joy.  In His name, Amen

*Andrea Helfrich*

## WOVEN TAPESTRIES

*O*ur Gracious and Loving Lord,
    We thank You. Father You have tugged at our heart strings and pulled them so very tight at times—to the point of pain, sorrow and ache; may we remember that You never fail to surround us with Your warmth of love and protection through any trial. Only when we come to our knees and seek Your Word are we filled with wonder, fear, concern, hope and excitement. Faith will help to shape us and, therefore, we will be renewed through each day. When we seek to make sense of the senseless, help us, guide us and enable us to seek our treasure in Your word.

    We are all here for Your own purpose, Lord. We thank You for the ways we have each grown, shared and learned, strengthening the bonds of woven tapestries each of us has made with You in our walk as Christians. May we each step out of the boat knowing You are our life preserver. The more intimately we know You, the more buoyant we become each day, no matter what we face. Help us to be willing to obey, to adjust ourselves, to listen and to serve You. Help us keep You at the center of our lives each day; realizing we can do nothing apart from You. Lord let us please see the world through Your eyes and let others see You in us. Amen

*Indi Cesari*

# GOD'S HOLY SPIRIT AND PRAYER

*T*he two are inseparable: As God speaks to us through His Word, we can speak to God in our prayers. 1 Peter 1:8 states, "Though you have not seen Him, you love Him, and even though you do not see Him now, you believe in Him and are filled with an inexpressible and glorious joy." We can respond to God with praise and thanksgiving for His encouraging words to us. The more we read of Him from His Holy Word, the more clearly and more deeply we can know Him. God also speaks to us in our thoughts as we meditate in prayer, even while listening and waiting for His revelation. Psalm 37:4 states: "Delight yourself in the Lord and He will give you the desires of your heart." As He enters our hearts by the power of His Spirit, He guides us into His Truth (John 16:13). His desires become our own. Thus we can clearly understand and appreciate His words in John 15:7, "If You remain in me and my words remain in you, ask whatever you wish, and it will be given you."

Dear Heavenly Father, all glory, honor, splendor and blessings be Yours and to Your Son Jesus Christ, my

Savior and Lord. Father, You are the Eternal, Almighty King of Heaven and earth. Thank You for revealing Yourself in Jesus and for Your forgiveness through Him. By Your Holy Spirit's power You give me wisdom and knowledge for every detail of my life. You, Dear Jesus, are the Faithful One and Only True Living God. "For Your Word is living and active, sharper than any double-edged sword. It penetrates even to dividing soul and spirit, joints and marrow; it judges the thoughts and attitudes of the heart. Nothing in all creation is hidden from Your sight. Everything is uncovered and laid bare before You to whom we must give account." (Hebrews 4:12,13).

Father, thank You for Your Word and for the power of Your Holy Spirit, who is the Living Truth, Jesus Christ, who teaches me to pray. Thank You for the privilege of being a member of the Women's Community Bible Study. Thank You for leading me by Your grace and showing me how to serve You. Please strengthen and guide us in Your Truth as we study Your Holy Word and learn to pray for Your Kingdom. Please prepare us, Lord God, to "answer anyone who asks us to give the reason for the hope that we have" and help us to "do this with gentleness and respect." (1 Peter 3:15)  May Your thoughts and words become our own as we persevere to be more like Jesus Christ.

In His Name, Amen


*B.J. Fisher*

# A PRAYER FOR DAILY LIVING

*D*ear Lord,
Help me to remember that there are no coincidences in life.

The small surprises and chance encounters we experience are Your ways of speaking to us. You are gently nudging us to open our eyes, to acknowledge Your presence in our lives, and to respond to Your will. You are tapping us on the shoulder to awaken us to new opportunities and challenges that may, if acted upon, enrich our lives and the lives of those we meet. If I am centered in Christ and fully aware of every moment you give me, then I will not miss Your lessons, Your guidance, Your quiet voice. I will not miss an opportunity to witness for You, to dry a tear, to be a source of strength in a time of weakness, to reach out and share Your love, to be a touchstone of light.

If I listen, You will speak to me. If I invite You, You will come to me. And if I remember Your eternal promise, "Lo, I am with you always," life's serendipities will be made into blessings. Amen

*Sheila H. Shessel*

*C*onsider it all joy, my brethren, when you encounter various trials, knowing that the testing of Your faith produces endurance.  And let endurance have its perfect result, that You may be perfect and complete, lacking in nothing." (James 1:2-4)

Lord, You know I don't like words like "trials" and "testing" and "endurance." They make me uncomfortable.  Oh, I know James was writing to the church in times of great persecution, but doesn't this verse speak to us today as well? What day passes that does not have its share of little trials that we have to endure? Many of us have days when trials seem overwhelming, but generally, our trials are the disappointments of the day, or irritating inconveniences, or the things that happen to us beyond our control. Those little trials tend to mount up and by the end of the day their sum total envelopes us with fatigue and discouragement.

Lord, I was hoping that when I became a Christian my trials would be over, but You never said that, did You? Trials come to Christians and non-Christians alike. So how should God's children respond to trials?

O Lord, I want to respond correctly to life's trials. I want to remember Your many promises like, "All things work together for good to those who love God and are called according to His purposes." (Romans 8:28) I want to remember that You have told us through Paul, "To be anxious for nothing, but in all things with prayer, and supplication, and thanksgiving we are to make our request known to You, and You will give us Your peace that passes all understanding." (paraphrase of Phil 4:6-7) I want to remember that Christ Himself said that "in this world we will have tribulation, but to be of good cheer for He has overcome the world." (paraphrase of John 16:33)

"Be of good cheer..."

"Consider it all joy...

Lord, if I can't remember anything else in times of trouble, by the power of Your Spirit, bring all Your wonderful promises to mind so that I may have peace and joy and be of good cheer. O Lord, I thank You for Your promises that comfort me in the good times and the bad. I can even look back now and thank You for the various trials of my life because as uncomfortable and even painful as they have been, I can see that the testing of my faith stretched my faith and did help me to endure.  Lord, I don't know what tomorrow will bring, but I know You will be there. As my faith is stretched, You will help me endure so that one day I will, as James says... "Be complete, lacking in nothing," and I will then truly consider it all joy.

Thank You, Lord. Amen

*D.D. Cardwell*

# A SACRED COVENANT

*M*y little sister got married yesterday. I watched her filled with excitement, nervousness, butterflies and a sense of anticipation of the unknown that lay before her. I have witnessed the friendship and love that has grown between this couple and has now blossomed into this moment of the marriage vows. I know because of their commitment to God, Jesus, the Holy Spirit and each other that this marriage will last. It will endure with God in control, the good and bad times, the troubled and joy-filled ones, the lean and abundant times, the births and the deaths.

Our lives should emulate this. We have a marriage with our Heavenly Father. We joined together as one with Him when we invited Him into our lives and gave our hearts, souls, minds and bodies to become a vessel for Him. Because we cannot see Him standing beside us every moment of every day, we sometimes forget our marriage vows and let other "things" replace Him in our lives.

Lord, help us to always see the love in Your eyes, as we first did when we gave ourselves to You. Amen

*Jill Cadenhead*

# A PRAYER OF THANKSGIVING

*F*ather, God of all goodness,
As we enter this season of Thanksgiving, we thank
You and bless You that You have loved us with an
everlasting love.

This morning, we come before You, most grate-
fully acknowledging the gift of motherhood and the lives
of the precious children You have entrusted to our care.

For the first steps, the sleepless nights, and
mashed bananas in their hair, we thank You.

For the bouquet of wildflowers offered in a tiny
hand, we thank You.

For the carpools, the dinosaur projects, the
birthday parties, we thank You.

From, "Mom, I wrecked the car," to, "Mom, I got
into college," we thank You. For now we have tasted
Your experience in parenting us.

Lord, make us each a channel of Your love to our
children. For in us they will see an abundant and
unconditional love or measured affection: a joyful
availability, or "come back later," love spelled T-I-M-E or
"get someone else to help you." In us they will see Christ
or they will not.

Father, God, may we do unto our children as You in Christ, have done unto us.

In His Holy Name, we pray. Amen

*Janet Burrell*

## LOVE AND FELLOWSHIP

*D*ear friends, let us love one another, for love comes from God.. Everyone who loves has been born of God and knows God. Whoever does not love does not know God, because God is love." 1 John 4:7,8

Heavenly, most gracious Father,

I give thanks to You for all of the loving friendships in my life. You have blessed all of us with Your love, and from Your love, we are able to love others. I think of my family and of all the friendships that have passed in and out of my life through the years. I think of all that has been taught me and of all the ways in which I have been loved and supported. It is from these friends and through their love that I have come to know about You.

The different experiences, outlooks and interests of these people have shown me how loving, compassionate, forgiving and good You are. As I share in the lives of my friends, I learn about joy, discipline, humility, grief, prayer, handling life's "curve balls" and so much more. They teach me how truly divine You are to have created us all so differently. Each of us has been created to bring something unique to the table of life's journeys. It is during the intimate moments of getting to know one another in friendships that we learn so much about life and we come to see You more clearly day-by-day. Lord, when You create fellowship for us, You create a glorious way to personally experience Your love, as well as to spread it. I give You thanks, Lord, for all the seeds that my friends plant in my soul, whether knowingly or not, that bring me closer to You. I pray that our friendships will be kind and compassionate, that we will use choice words to uplift, encourage, teach and admonish one another. Lord, I pray that we will be more grateful for our relationships than our accomplishments. And, Lord, I pray that when You want to teach me something new or when You want to move in my life, that I will be sensitive to You. I give thanks, Dear Lord, for friends, and fellowship and pray that we will all be centered in Christ.

Dear Lord, I love You. Amen

*Margaret Young*

# UNIFIED IN A DESIRE TO KNOW CHRIST

*D*ear Father,
   Since You are the initiator of a loving relationship with us, our high and holy calling is to respond to Your offer. And so today, we come with grateful hearts to grow closer to You through the study of Your Word through prayer, and through fellowship.

   As we leave our busy agendas this morning to come to this special place, quiet our hearts and minds and allow us to hear what we have been called to hear and to be obedient to Your Word.

   We all come from many different places in our spiritual journeys with You, and we rejoice today in our diversity. Yet we are unified in our desire to know Christ in a personal way.

   As we grow in Your Grace, enhance our capacity to respond to one another with humility, gentleness, patience, and with love.

   Thank You for Your unconditional love and Your acceptance of each of us. You are our Strength, our Hope, our Comforter, our Counselor and our Friend. Amen

*Pam Elting*

*D*ear Heavenly Father,
  We've come today seeking to know You, to love You, to believe You, to trust You and to obey You. Oftentimes we fail to do this. Our focus should be on You and we should be an example of Christ living in us. We give praise to Your Holy name and ask for forgiveness of our sins, forgiveness of our failed intentions, and forgiveness for our disobedience. You gave us life and we seek to do Your will here on earth as is in Heaven. With our hearts and actions working together, we pray Your plan will be accomplished.

  In Christ's name we pray and thank You for letting us have a second chance to obey and trust You. Amen

*Linda Elliot*

# WE ARE NEVER LOST TO HIS SPIRIT

*L*et us pray together:
Father, as we gather here in this quiet moment
we thank You,
we praise You
that You are the living God.
Before anything else existed,
You were there,
You are here now,
and You will always be.
We thank You that You are a good and powerful God
and that You love us all the time.
As the Psalmist says in Psalm 139
You know when we stand or sit,
You know our every thought,
You know each moment where I am,
even what I will say before I say it.
This is so glorious God —
we can never be lost to Your Spirit.

How extraordinary to know that you are thinking
about each one of us constantly!

When the troubles of the day come crashing in on
us like a tidal wave Lord,

let us remember how You quieted the waves in the midst of the storm
and saved the boat from sinking.
Give us faith that is not choked out by the thorns of worry, riches or needs,
the responsibilities or pleasures of life.
Keep us focused on You, Lord,
that our faith may constantly grow in fertile soil
nourished by the words and teachings of other believers
and  each one of  us as we minister one to the other.
Let Your Holy Spirit be present within each of our hearts today.
In Your Son Jesus' Holy Name we pray.
Amen

*Betsy B. Weitnauer*

# A PRAYER OF THANKS IN TIME OF GRIEF

*D*ear Gracious, Heavenly Father,
    Thank You for all the blessings of this life.
Thank You especially for the gift of Your Son, Our
Saviour, Jesus Christ, so that we can be made perfect in
Your sight and be brought into a relationship with You.
Thank You for the gift of Your Holy Spirit, the Great
Comforter, who has made Your presence and love
known to me during this time of great sorrow over the
loss of my husband, the father of our two young sons.
You have been at work preparing my heart in many
ways for the terrible news of his untimely death. You
have given me strength and courage to go on with a new
awareness of Your precious gifts.

    Thank You for our joy, that surpasses all under-
standing, as we mourn our loss, and for Your promise to
provide for our every need. Father, I ask Your blessings
upon the many friends who have prayed for us and
showered us with love and kindness. Lord, give us the
opportunity to share Your love with others as You have
poured out Your love on us.

    Father, we remember my husband today on what

would have been his 51st birthday and thank you for his life. I pray that somehow through his death Your name will be glorified.

In Christ's precious name. Amen

*Sandra Carey*

# A PRAYER FOR MY CHILD

Dear God,
Thank You for my child,
For she is such a blessed gift!
I pray for wisdom and guidance
As she grows in my care.
Help me to remember that she is my teacher, as well.
For we experience You more fully through our children.
As we learn and grow from each other:
Let me show her unconditional love, so that she will always seek the highest good.
Let me show faith, that she may accept Your words: "I am the Life and the Way, follow Me."
Let me show honesty, that she may know to always speak the truth.
Let me show forgiveness, that she may learn to live by Your grace.
Let me show commitment, that she may find the strength to stay on course.
Let me show Christ in my living, that she may feel Your constant presence.

Let me show compassion, that she might awaken to know the gift of service.

Let me show encouragement as she grows and seeks safe passage through new territories of life.

Let me live in gratitude to You for my daughter, that she may understand the joys of being a child of God.

Amen

*Sheila H. Shessel*

# *SEEING EACH OTHER WITH CHRISTIAN EYES*

*O*Heavenly Father, we come to You this morning with grateful hearts: grateful for this time of fellowship and worship and grateful for Your amazing grace, which is available to every one of us. As we continue to study the book of Ephesians, help us to understand that Paul speaks to us today as clearly as he spoke to the Ephesians centuries ago.

Like the early Christians, help us to fully understand that Christ, Your Son, is living and working within each of us as we entrust our lives to Him. Help us to feel Your abundant love which surrounds us today and every day that we may feel filled with the Holy Spirit, strengthened to do Your will, and to put Christ, not ourselves, first in our lives.

Help us, O Lord, to take time every day to quiet our minds and slow down our activities that we may take a moment to pray to You, God the Father. It is in prayer that we feel close to You and can talk to You and can share our joys, our triumphs, our sorrows and disappointments. Like the ever-patient and loving Father that You are to us, Your special children, You lift the burden of our worries from our souls and in its place fill us with love and serenity that we may face the challenges to come as opportunities to serve You. We are fortified with the knowledge that You are by our side, guiding us throughout the day.

This morning, as we come together as friends, help us to see one another with Christian eyes full of love and hearts full of fellowship. Help us to recognize the special talents and gifts that You have bestowed upon each of us. Sometimes we feel inadequate, that we have no special talents and are unsure of ourselves. Help us to remember that talent includes any ability we might have to enrich the lives of those around us, that we all have the talent to be a friend, to give others our time, our attention, our help and our support. We have the talent to listen, to comfort and to love.

And so, Dear God the Father, God the Son, and God the Holy Spirit, open our hearts that we may feel the joy of Jesus in our souls as we pray together the prayer He taught us long ago [The Lord's Prayer]. Amen.

*Laura Blackburn*

# HE TALKS TO ME

When I'm alone
Afraid of the unknown
Lost, can't find my way
He answers me
In His time and in His way

He talks to me
Through everyone I meet
He talks to me
Gives to me a dream
And if I listen to His voice
I'm not alone to make the choice
He talks to me
He talks to you
He talks to me

He's always there
To answer your prayer
But the miracle begins with you
Just ask the Lord
He'll find the way

To guide you through your darkest day
He'll talk to you
Through everyone you meet
He'll talk to you
Give to you a dream
And if you listen to His voice
You're not alone to make the choice
He talks to you
He talks to me
He talks to me

He can lighten heavy loads
Lift your heart from deep despair
Remember you are not alone
Through the power of prayer!

He talks to me
Through everyone I meet
He talks to me
Gives to me a dream
And I  listen to His voice

I'm not alone to make the choice
He talks to me
He talks to you
He talks to me!
Amen

*Song written and published by Mary Welch Rogers*

# ENABLE US TO BE A BLESSING TO OUR WORLD

*D*ear Precious Father,
We come to You with grateful hearts today. Enable us to be a blessing to our world. As we begin each day, as mothers, sisters, daughters, friends, wives, neighbors, career women, Christians...equip us to be a light to others.

Give us the desire to surrender our lives to You daily, Lord. Move into our hearts and make Your home there. Give us Your eyes to see. Empower us to be the best that we can be, glorifying You in all that we are and do. We pray earnestly today that You will enable us to genuinely place our needs for security and significance in You. May we grow as sisters in Christ, secure in the knowledge of Your love, Your acceptance of us, Your sovereignty, and Your constant presence in our lives always. Amen

*Pam Elting*

## LEGACIES OF LOVE

*D*uring the past several months, my husband's mother and father died following lengthy, debilitating illnesses. Their lovely, old home was placed on the market and my husband and I went by regularly to assure things remained in order. We came to dread those visits because the house that had been such a hub of activity for nearly forty years was now just an empty shell. Our grief over the loss of two such vital family members was overwhelming. There no longer seemed to be any energy in the house—or in us!

One lovely spring day, while standing in their living room, sunlight streamed through the old paned windows, permeating everything with the most beautiful, golden glow. It felt as though the energy that had been so evident in the past had returned and was suffusing the room. My husband and I believe that God had a message for us in that moment, at a time when we were feeling so depleted. For after that day, we became increasingly aware that none of their material possessions were of lasting value. But the spirit and vitality of his parents were indestructible. The extraordinary integrity of his father and the exemplary loyalty of his mother were permanently interwoven into the fabric of our own family. And the greatest legacy of all was my mother-in-law's deep, unshakable faith in God and His omnipotent presence in all things, good or tragic.

Heavenly Father, we thank You for Your divine, often unrecognized presence during the most devastating of life's trials. We are so deeply grateful for Your healing power that never fails when we are at our lowest ebb. Please keep us faithful to Your divine plan. Give us the courage to live according to Your will. Amen

*Marianne Craft*

## WE REJOICE IN DOING HIS WILL

*D*ear Heavenly Father,
We come to You with joy and thanksgiving in our hearts. We are blessed in so many ways. We thank You for Your faithfulness and constant love. We thank You for all our wonderful leaders, who weekly through their ministries, help each one of us to grow in our faith and to understand that doing Your will is a daily process to embrace and rejoice in. Help each one of us, in our materialistic worlds, to focus on the *forever* and not the *now*, knowing in our hearts that the *good life now* comes from a strong faith and from acting on our faith.

As we study about making adjustments and being called into obedience, help us to understand what Paul meant when he said, "Obedience results from a relationship with You." *Obedience* will never, in and of itself, create or earn that relationship.

We want to strengthen our relationship with You. We remain ever grateful for your diligence in showing us, through Your Word, in our prayers, and by many circumstances, how to better hear You and to then know Your will. In Your precious name we pray. Amen

*Cathy Masterson*

*D*earest Heavenly Father,
You are truly such an awesome God, amazing in every way! It is such a privilege to be able to come before You and pour out our hearts to You with our praises, our thanksgivings, and our requests. We have so much to be thankful for: this Bible study that is truly Yours, the wonderful group of women that gather to learn more about You, the friendships that have formed with You at the center, your unconditional, agape love, Your guidance and direction, Your wisdom that is there for the asking, Your incredible Word that is our instruction book for life, Your beautiful creation, and, most of all, for the gift of Your Son. Through our relationship with Christ, we have the incredible gifts of forgiveness, daily guidance, and eternal life. We are so blessed! Thank You, Father, for all that You are and for allowing us to be a part of Your Kingdom! Continue to give us the desire to know You more intimately, to spend time with You daily, and enable us to honor You in all of our choices, decisions, and relationships. We thank You again for Your many, many blessings. In Jesus' Name, Amen

*Hyland Justice*

# HUMBLE SURRENDER

*H*eavenly Father,
We thank You, Lord, for being a loving and gracious Father who cares for each one of us.

Give us the grace to deny ourselves and take up our cross and follow You. We humbly surrender our mind, will, body, emotions and life to You, Master, and ask that You forgive our sins.

Lord, fill us with Your Holy Spirit that gives us knowledge of truth and understanding of Your will, rest for our souls and power to do Your work.

Remind us to trust You to direct us in all we do and to plan our daily work under Your leadership.

Father, we ask that You bless our plans and help us to depend on You to direct our actions. Give us the discipline we need to carry out Your ways and give us the faith to leave the results of our actions to You, O Lord.

Thank You for using us as a living sacrifice. In Jesus Name, Amen

*Jennifer Egbert*

# A DESIRE TO BE VICTORS

*G*od, help us as we strive to know You through the written word in the Bible. Teach us to accept Your message, although we may not always understand or have all the answers to our questions. Help our faith and trust in You to grow, to bridge those gaps (those gray areas), where answers and full understanding sometimes evade us.

Enable us to focus on You and help us perfect our relationship with You. Decrease our desire to be perfect in this world. Help us to let go of self and our earthly focus. Rather than be victims of others, show us how to be victors in Christ.

*Joanie Michaels*

# A PRAYER FOR DIVINE STRESS MANAGEMENT

*A*s I was running this morning, I was thinking about how we so often run from spending time alone with God. We can come up with all sorts of valid reasons — we gave them all when we were trying to put this little book together. At the top of the list — "busy-ness." We're so busy. No time, how sad. Layers of busyness just get added to the layer of other stresses which are already pretty constant companions to most of us.

How do we handle all this stress? Some of us walk, some of us run, some of us eat too much, some of us drink too much, some of us shop too much, some of us yell too much and some of us just get busier.

I picture God with a divinely soft and heavenly sofa waiting for me. He motions for me to come lie down and still myself. He tells me he knows how to handle stress, that He is in fact the Divine Stress Manager. He should be; He lived with stress daily. He talks to me about how He always withdrew to His wilderness and prayed — in the good times and the bad. He tells me to turn to my Bible and to renew my mind with His promises in Philippians 4: 6-8: "Don't worry, instead pray about everything — if you do this you will experience God's peace which is far more wonderful than the human mind can understand. His peace will keep your thoughts and your hearts quiet and at rest as you trust in Christ Jesus."

Dear Lord,
You know our fears, our anxieties, our hesitations and You know the crutches we have developed to handle them. Forgive us for not letting You be the One on whom we lean and to whom we are addicted. Help us each to want to find our knees more often. Help us to see prayer as a beautiful therapy available to each of us at anytime. Lord, above all else, help us each to realize that we don't have the time not to pray. Amen

*Linda Wyatt*

## WE SEEK YOU IN ALL THINGS

*L*ord Jesus Christ,
We come before You at this special time each week seeking Your face. When first You came into this world, it was as a suffering servant; You were a man of sorrows and acquainted with grief. Help us to remember as we face the trials and temptations in our own lives that there is nothing You have not experienced, no feeling You have not felt. You seek to refine and purify us, so that when we ultimately stand before the Father, with You at our side, we can hear Him say, "Well done, thou good and faithful servant."

Save us from the curse of the charmed life. Let not our good fortune and our good health make us immune and unfeeling toward the wounded, the weary and the weak; for at some time during our lives, we will be all of these.

In the words of my pastor*, "Give us enough tears to keep us tender, enough hurts to keep us human, enough failure to keep our hands tightly in Your own, and enough success to make us certain we walk with You." You have promised that in refining us, if we are not delivered *out* of the fire, You will walk with us *through* the fire.

May our tears teach us compassion, our pain teach us empathy and our failure teach us humility and obedience, so that our lives may be used for Your purpose, and we may become Your hands and Your heart in this place.

In Your Holy Name we pray. Amen

*Janet Burrell*

*\*Asa Meadows, pastor, Covenant Presbyterian Church, Augusta, Georgia*

## *YOU COMMAND US TO LOVE*

*D*ear Heavenly Father,
You are wonderful, O Lord. Thank You for the love and care You give me. I know that You love me because You sent Your Son to be my Savior. He showed me how to love You and love others.

I want to obey Your command to love You with all my heart and soul and mind and to love my neighbor as myself. I want to show others about Your love and how much I love You by the way I love them. Please grant me the power through the Holy Spirit to demonstrate mercy, kindness, humility, patience, gentleness and forgiveness to others in all of my relationships. Amen

*Mary Inman*

# A PRAYER TO HEAR HIS VOICE

*F*ather, our Father,
I praise You. I thank You that we are Your children and can come into Your Presence. You, Creator of the universe, who placed the stars from Your fingers, know our name. I bless You and magnify Your name. Thank You for giving us Your Son, Jesus, and the gentle Holy Spirit to walk with us, to lead and guide us in this strange land that is not our home. I praise You; for all good things come from You.

I lift up to You all those in need today: the wounded, the poor, the hungry and those in need of a Savior. Father, touch us and show us how to let You live through us to meet their needs. Father, give us ears to hear Your voice saying, "This is the Way, walk you in it." We ask for grace to be like Jesus, to complete the task You have given us today, not to be hard-hearted and go our own way. Instead let us come into the rest and cease from our own labors.

Thank You that You humble Yourself and bend down from Heaven to listen and answer our cry. May we always pray the prayers on the heart of Jesus, who lives to intercede for us. In His Precious Name, Amen

*Paula Smith*

## *FOCUSING ON WHAT MATTERS*

*H*eavenly Father,
   The last fast-paced days of the school year are
filled with baseball championship games, chorus oldies
concerts, graduation dances, field days and birthday
party celebrations to name just a few. Most of us know
the elements that fill the slots in the calendar pages. The
time is fleeing by, Lord. I have held each of my infants'
frail heads as they nestled against my chest feeling
intensely warm and secure. Now I am watching each
child walking tall, taking each step in faith with Your
unconditional love and a mother's love, as they grow
each day.

   Suddenly a bolt of reality, reminding us of our
mortality, hits when a close friend discovers that a case
of tonsillitis is rediagnosed as throat cancer. Wait! Those
calendar appointments don't seem to matter right now;
a close friend needs me more. You, Lord, are calling us
to focus on Your priorities and not the multitude of
daily distractions. As we stand in a circle, our hands
clasped in prayer, our friend's cancer surgery begins in
the operating room below. Each of us feels the Holy
Spirit cover our fears with peace. We are empowered by

you when we feel we cannot cope or hope. So, the countless days with their complicated itineraries and plans, the unexpected crises that come and go, are all in your hands. If we can just follow You, You will lead us home. Thank you for the honor of believing in You and being loved by You. Amen

*Indy Cessari*

## *LET YOUR LIGHT SHINE IN US*

*O*ur Heavenly Father,
We sing praises to Your holy name. In our quiet time, when we retreat from the clamor, noise and bustle of our routine, we feel Your presence. We delight in the beauty of Your creation — bright sunlight falling on the trees, birds chirping, fresh scents in the air. Your arms are stretched wide to receive us, and we long for the comfort You alone can provide.

We acknowledge that we sin and fall short of the Glory of God. We pray for Your forgiveness.

Father, we pray, let Your light shine in us, wherever we are, for others to see. Whether we're driving carpool, riding in carpool, sitting in class at school, playing sports with friends, being with brother or sisters, parents or children, keep us ever mindful that we are Your hands and feet on earth. Keep our ears tuned to Your message; keep our eyes on Your face and attentive to Your words in Holy Scripture.

As You have commanded, let us love You and our fellow man. May we abound in the fruits of the Spirit: love, joy, peace, patience, kindness, goodness, faithfulness, gentleness and self-control.

We thank You, Father, for the countless blessings You have bestowed upon us. How wonderful that nothing can separate us from Your love.

We pray without ceasing. Amen

*Sue Clineburg and her daughter Melissa, age 13*

# *A PRAYER TO SHAPE US AND MOLD US*

*H*eavenly Father,
There are over a hundred beautiful heads here this morning, each one bowed before you, God. We, who met at the foot of the cross, come before You to be still and know that You are God, and to commune with You, soul to soul. Father, how deeply You love us. Will we ever in this lifetime comprehend the depth, the passion, the integrity and the endurance of that love? You hold us in Your heart, and as we seek You, we will come to know that there is a place there for each of us.

Tune our ears to hear You, Lord. Develop in us such childlike trust that in all the circumstances of life—joy, grief, disappointment, failure and death—we look up to You, knowing that Yours is the love that will not let us go. Out of it You shape us to be holy and formed in the likeness of Christ. That the potter should die for the clay is an amazing thought.

Walk beside us today, let Your hand rest upon each one gently as a benediction, such that we never forget who and whose we are. In the Name of our Lord and Savior, Jesus Christ, Amen

*Janet Burrell*

# A PRAYER TO STILL OURSELVES

*D*ear God,
Help us to quiet our minds and remove ourselves from the busy activities of our day so we can hear You. Remove us briefly from our temporal world, our world of self, and help us focus on You for the spiritual relationship we so desperately need.

Guide us, direct us and constantly remind us that You are in control. You are there for us and we can experience Your joy and love by seeking Your forgiveness of our sins.

Be with us, Your loving servants.
In Jesus Christ we pray, Amen.

*Joanie Michaels*

# IN PRAISE OF GOD'S WORD

*D*ear Holy Father,
God of all Creation, God of eternal hope, love, and truth in and through Your Son, Jesus Christ. To You, Jehovah — Jesus be all glory, praise, and honor forever and ever. You conquered sin and death on the cross. You are the risen, Living God, in whom I have been forgiven. I know you live in my heart by the power of Your Holy Spirit. You give understanding of your Holy Word to every believer who hungers and thirsts for Your truth. Thank You for Your words: "Do your best to present yourself to God as one approved, a workman who does not need to be ashamed and who correctly handles the word of truth." 2 Timothy 2:15.

You enable us and equip us with Your Spirit's motivation to intercede for the lost and those in need, praying in Your love and in Your truth. Father, inspire me to new heights as I strive to live your promises: "I thank Christ Jesus our Lord who has given me strength, that He considered me faithful, appointing me to His service." 1 Timothy 1:12.

Following Paul's example in his letter to Timothy, may we abide in Your blessings through Jesus Christ. In The Name of Jesus, Amen

*B.J. Fisher*

# MAY WE RADIATE YOUR LOVE

*F*ather God,
As we gather here in Your presence to be filled with the love and grace of Your Son, Jesus Christ, bless our leaders, our members, and our mission. As surely as Your spirit fills each and every aspect of our lives, allow us to be receptors of that spirit, and transformers of it in our dealings with others. It is not the great moments of our lives that we remember in the quiet of our souls, those decorative, public, official events that seem so all-consuming on our calendars. Rather, it is the unexpected moments of love, the hugs, the quick tear of joy or compassion, the lump in our throats when we find ourselves unable to join in (with our voices) a hymn that moves our emotions, yet find our hearts singing. Thank You Lord, for the spaces in our lives that are filled with your love. Surround us with Your Spirit, and let us see it not as the delicate strands of a gossamer web as we travel through life, but love as gentle and all encompassing as the rays of the sun, non-discriminating, non-judgmental and available to us all. May we radiate Your love through our actions to those we encounter, and to those we love. In Jesus' name we pray, Amen

*Tina Thompson*

# PRAYER FOR MY CHILDREN

*T*hank You, Father, for the gift of children. They are a delight and a joy. They teach us much about Your unconditional love and acceptance.

I pray that as my children grow older they will also grow in their desire to seek after You. I pray that they would hunger and thirst for You and that the hunger and thirst would not be quenched until they have an intimate love relationship with Jesus Christ. Please develop in them a bright light that others may see. May their lives touch hundreds of others because of their love for You and a desire to glorify You. I pray that You would bind Satan from their lives and give them the power and strength to resist temptation. Please bless them with Your wisdom and guidance. I pray that they would marry a mate who truly loves You and desires to honor You. Gracious Father, please be with them and strengthen them through the rough bumpy roads as well as the smooth ones. May they see Your hand daily and experience the peace that can only come from You.

Please guide me daily so that I can be a Christlike example for them. Help me to impart Your wisdom and love to them. Please give me patience and understanding when I do not feel I have it to give. Keep a humble heart in me, O Lord. Please give me the discernment to know when I should ask for forgiveness from them. Help me to be the parent you want me to be so that they can be all you desire them to be.

In Your Blessed Name.

*Jeannie Ross*

# SEEKING GOD'S GUIDANCE

*O*ur Gracious Heavenly Father,
We come to You today in the start of a New Year with renewed faith, hope, and a sincere desire to do Your Will. We are filled with love and gratitude for the abundance of grace and mercy you constantly shower upon us all. We are thankful that You always provide for all of our needs. We praise Your name, and we are filled with awe that You sent Jesus Christ to earth from His exalted place in Heaven with You. He shares in our joys, our sorrows, our problems and anxieties. He teaches us how to live and shows us Your love. He died for each one of us, to redeem us and assure us of a place with Him in Your Kingdom for all eternity.

Presently, we come to this point in our study where the crisis of belief is a turning point in our lives where we must make a decision. Help us to live our lives every day so that we are testimonies of what we believe about You, that You are our first priority, and that we will be open and willing to follow You wherever You lead us. Give us the faith of Moses and Joshua, Gideon and David, Peter and Paul, and all of the other disciples.

When we encounter You, help us to respond with action and without hesitation.

We need You every hour of every day to sustain us, to pick us up when we falter, to love us when we fail, and to give us courage to stop doing things our way instead of listening for the voice which says: "Be still and know that I am God."

We ask Your blessing upon this dedicated group of women who earnestly seek Your will in their lives. And we ask that You lay Your healing hand upon and comfort all those who are going through trials of divorce, loss of job, financial problems, mental, physical or emotional illness, the homeless, and the poor. May we be there to help and care for all those in need.

In the precious and powerful name of Jesus Christ, our Lord, Savior, Redeemer, and Friend. Amen

*Mary McKee*

# *LEARNING TO LOVE UNCONDITIONALLY*

*A*lmighty God,
I come to You today in thanksgiving. As I move frantically through each day, I fail to remember it is You who are always there with me through thick and thin. No matter how undeserved I am, I always can look to You and know how much You love me and care for me. You are always there to pick me up, hold me and give me comfort. You always let me know I am not alone. You are beside me. Your unconditional love for me carries me through.

Teach me, O Father, to love unconditionally, to love and care for others with no expectations from them or for me. Guide me in letting go of all the stones that get in my way of truly loving others unconditionally. Take away the judgment, selfishness, pride and fear. Help me to love others unrelentingly as You love me. Help me share Your perfect love with all. This I humbly ask in your name.

*Nell Long*

# IN PRAISE OF HOLY SCRIPTURE

*D*ear Heavenly Father,
We praise You and we give you thanks for leaving us Your precious Word...the Bible.

I thank You Lord for being with us today and I thank You for calling each one of us to a closer more intimate relationship with You.

Lord, I pray that You will protect and bless us and our families as we begin this new year.

Lord, open our minds so that we may understand Your Word; open our lips so that we may proclaim Your Word; open the eyes of our hearts so that we may live and experience You through Your Word.

Father, give us the grace and the gifts that we need to know and do Your will. Lord, show us how to surrender everything to you. Show us how to die so that Your Son may live.

Lord, I pray that You will reveal Yourself to us through the power of Your Holy Spirit.

May all that we do bring You honor and glory.

I ask all of this in the precious name of our Savior and our Redeemer...Your Son, Jesus Christ. Amen

*Keri Allen*

# GOD'S LOVE AT WORK

*T*wenty or thirty volunteers stand in a rough semi-circle around the front porch of a newly built Habitat for Humanity home on Washington Street in South Atlanta. It is time to dedicate the house. It is time for it to become a home.

The dirty, sweaty volunteers, wearing their organization's t-shirts, are smiling and joyfully awaiting the simple ceremony where a family will, at last, touch the dream that has been only a distant thought for their entire life.

Several people speak, kind words are said, a plaque is given, and the family, dressed in their best clothes, wait nervously. They know the new owner will be asked to say something shortly. Finally, a Bible is handed to the homeowner with words about God's love in action. The Bible is taken in trembling hands with a quiet thank you, and then there is silence. The offer to speak gently prods the homeowner to the front, and, with children hanging on, the homeowner thanks her Jesus. All these years she has known that one day Jesus would answer her prayer and now He has. Her voice grows to almost a scream of joy as she praises her Lord for answering her prayer.

Her voice softens and almost inaudibly she thanks the volunteers for their work and love for her and her children. Crying, she steps back behind the others. The volunteers all clap and many share the homeowner's tears. All know that they have made a difference in the life of a family, that what just happened was good and Jesus was pleased.

"I tell you the truth, whatever you did for one of the least of these brothers of mine, you did for me." (Matthew 25:40)

*Judy Heald*

# *WITH OR WITHOUT HIM*

*S*everal years ago, I found myself timidly tiptoeing into Bible Study. I was somewhat of a doubter and thoroughly intimidated by the wiser friends around me. My spirit was a teachable one, though, and in this safe place of loving and accepting women, I was able to learn and grow in and with God's grace. I have learned that...

Christ's grace is sufficient enough for my blunders...

His forgiveness is awesome and complete...

His patience is unending...

His discipline is so necessary...

His direction is clear when I listen and am patient...

His timing is incredibly perfect...

His love for me and my love for others through Him are available at all times simply for the asking...

His provision when I rely on Him is so abundant and so assuredly from Him that my envy of others is gone...

My identity, when placed in Him, takes away my need to find security in things and definition by others...

What an abundant life! Not a perfect, carefree, or

problem free life, but certainly an abundant one! With or without Him? I've done it both ways — undoubtedly WITH HIM is my first choice! What a privilege to be a part of His kingdom!

*Hyland Justice*

## STOP, LOOK AND LISTEN

*T*oday, I came to work with my dad. His office is on the 14th floor of this building. It's really neat. While my dad sat and worked at his desk, I looked out the window into a massive and busy city. Cars were speeding along the roads and not stopping for other cars. Men were working on new tall buildings and I saw a train full of people rushing to get off. I'm afraid everyone is getting too caught up in material objects and not praising God to thank Him for all He has done. If You get too caught up in the world, just stop and think... you wouldn't be here if it wasn't for God. He watches over us and protects us and He is always with us when we need Him. We need to thank God for all He does for us.

One of my favorite verses reads, "Store up your treasures in Heaven, not on earth." Your life is like a minute compared to your eternal life in Heaven. Material things such as money or cars are many people's prized possessions, but when you get to Heaven these will have no value. The treasures that will be rewarded in Heaven will be given to those who have been kind, considerate, loving, and honest.

Dear Heavenly Father,

Please be with all of us throughout our days of work and help us remember to stop, look, and listen, and to store our treasures in Heaven and not on earth. Thank You! In Christ's Name, Amen

*Meggie McGuirk*
*Age 12*
*Daughter of Nancy McGuirk*

## YOU HEAR MY TINIEST WHISPER

*D*ear Heavenly Father,
You are the "Great I Am." Please give me the utmost desire to know you more. Little did I know that, through the most difficult circumstances, You desired a relationship with me. I have learned to trust You so You can work through me. Thank You for Your promise that I can do all things according to Your power that is within me. Waiting has brought me to my knees and has taught me patience and, most of all, to trust You in *all* things. Sometimes it seems I've waited so long for You to answer my prayer, knowing all along that You have heard my prayer. There are times I don't understand why You have taken so long to answer specific requests, even though I know You are working everything out for the best. In waiting, I've known that You have never forgotten about me. I've heard through my silence, "Wait." Even though I may have asked for something which is good. You have said in several instances, "You need to wait awhile, because You are not ready for it yet."

You hear and answer the prayers of Your children.

You see my tears and my smiles. You hear my tiniest whisper. How I thank You for choosing me and for giving me the blessings which are so abundant. You are an awesome God. Please help me now, Lord, to understand and to experience the joy and the peace that my answered prayers bring. I claim Your promise and know that if I ask anything according to Your will, You hear me and my prayers. When I trust that You hear me, I know that I have what I asked, whatever my request. Not my will, but Your will be done. As You also have promised, You will meet all of my needs according to Your glorious riches in Christ Jesus. God, be the glory forever and ever for the things You have done!

Lord, please also help me to set my mind on the things of the Spirit, seeking the things above (where You are seated), *not* on the things that are on this earth. Help me to be anxious for nothing, but by prayer and supplication, to praise You for all things, all the days of my life. Whatever is true, whatever is right, and honorable, whatever is pure, whatever is lovely, if there is any excellence, if anything is worthy of praise, *please* let my mind dwell on these things. Please guard my heart and my mind from evil, in Your name Christ Jesus.

How can I thank you for the things You have done for me? To You, Father God, be the glory. Amen

*Nancie Merrill*

# A PRAYER FOR CHILDREN

*O*ne of my favorite prayers to pray, especially for my children, is straight from Ephesians 3:16-19: "I pray that out of His glorious riches He may strengthen you with power through His Spirit in your inner being, so that Christ may dwell in your hearts through faith. And I pray that you, being rooted and established in love, may have power, together with all the saints, to grasp how wide and long and high and deep is the love of Christ, and to know this love that surpasses knowledge — that you may be filled to the measure of all the fullness of God."

*Gayle Nix*

# THE GREATEST GIFT

*I* will never forget our first family devotional. It would have been a great entry into America's funniest home videos.

Picture this. Around the dinner table, a squirmy three year old, a teething one year old, a very suspicious husband and an overly enthusiastic mother who had cleverly planned a ten minute lesson (that was way too long). You can only imagine how much attention I got.

Now let's take a step back. This meeting did not happen easily. After several fruitless suggestions to my husband about how wonderful it would be for us to have a family time with God each week, I became desperate. I prayed for God's timing and my patience. Finally, my husband and I cut a deal. He would sit through this weekly ritual if I would begin an exercise program (I said I was desperate).

So these first family devotionals were based on a lot of behind the scenes work. Anyway, we made it through that first lesson, and then it was time to pray (and I don't mean a blessing). My sweet husband who would far prefer to keep his faith private than to have it poured out over the dinner table, clinched my fist tightly and closed his eyes as if we were about to jump off a cliff...and said, "do it...do it!" So I quickly took my command and said a brief prayer. Sheeeeew! We made it; everyone was still alive. Mission accomplished!

As we all approached the next week nervously, it was actually much easier. In fact, as the weeks and months went by, we quickly grew to enjoy this time together.

Fast forward ten years and two more kids later. Today my husband and I will tell you that the most meaningful time that we have with our children is during these weekly devotionals. Now our thirteen and eleven year olds read the lesson (that Mom picked out), Dad asks all the questions to make sure everyone is listening, the nine and seven year olds read scriptures, and finally everyone takes a turn saying an open prayer to thank God for his many blessings and to ask Him for specific needs.

The GREATEST GIFT that God has given us is the gift of a relationship with Him made possible through His Son. Therefore, I believe the GREATEST GIFT that we can pass on to our children is to model the love of

Christ and to teach them about Christ. It is in fact a command from God. He does, after all, love them even more than we do. It's easy to depend on the churches or the schools to teach our children about the future, but the seeds of faith are rooted when planted at home. As we think about the future, what comfort it is to know that when we are gone, our children will be able to handle the valleys of life because of their trust and love in Jesus.

I am so grateful to God for His love, for my family and for God's help in keeping a husband faithful to his part of the deal. Now, as far as my exercise goes, well that's another story.

*Nancy McGuirk*

# OUR LORD PROVIDES COMFORT IN ALL

*I*t was two a.m. when my eyes popped open and the tossing and turning which accompanies worry began. In the morning, we would take our oldest child to camp for the first time — for a two-week session! For over twenty minutes my mind raced and I imagined every horrible thing that could possibly happen to a child while away at camp. She might drown, a wild animal might eat her, she might ride in a car without a seat belt—the list went on and on!

Finally, I was moved to get out of bed and pray, with the Bible close at hand. I prayed and searched the index under worry and protection. God led me to begin reading in Proverbs—and there it was—the comfort I knew He would provide!

Proverbs 3:21-26 "Have two goals: wisdom—that is, knowing and doing right—and common sense. Don't let them slip away, for they fill you with living energy and bring you honor and respect. They keep you safe from defeat and disaster and from stumbling off the trail. With them on guard, you can sleep without fear; you need not be afraid of disaster or the plots of wicked men, for the Lord is with you; He protects you."

All I had to do was use common sense regarding the Lord. He loves our children more than we as parents do. He will take care of them and comfort them just as He has taken care of and comforted me. More importantly, I was reminded again that worry is so unnecessary. No matter what pain we feel in our heart, no matter what causes that lump in our throat, no matter what keeps us awake at night—He is in control and He loves us. We are all children of God and can live in the wisdom of His provision and His faithfulness. Our job is to give our concerns to the Lord and leave them with Him in the knowledge of His love.

*Anne Trulock*

## HE WALKS BESIDE ME ALWAYS

*L*ord, you are so awesome. When I walked into my first day of high school, I looked around and realized what great opportunities God has given me. Too often, I take so many things for granted, Lord. I seem to look at the bad in my life and not the good. "Think positive and be confident of God's love," my mom always tells me, "and He will do the rest." He has given me wonderful friends, a great family and home, and a great education.

Before today, I was dreading high school. Being a ninth grader frightened me: the homework, difficult teachers, problems with friends and a lot more. But I prayed about it long and hard. I walked into school with my head up, thanking God for all the wonderful people and blessings in my life. Without Jesus Christ in my life, I wouldn't have anyone to thank. He walks beside me always and I felt him near today. I can thank Him for our special relationship...my friend and my Savior.

*Lindsay Elting*
*Age 15*
*Daughter of Pam Elting*

# HE IS TRULY THE LOVE OF MY LIFE

When my oldest child died five years ago I felt certain that God had a very specific purpose for my life and that it was somehow related to William's death. I remember kneeling in the chapel at Grady Hospital saying to God, "A child of mine is gone. I have a tremendous void in my life right now. Please, Lord, show me how to fill this void." I was searching for a task, a mission that God was going to give me. Every situation that arose, every person that came into my life, every new day I examined and questioned, maybe this is the "something" that is going to help heal, fill and complete my life. None of these were the answer to my prayers. A couple of years later my family and I moved to Pawleys Island. It was quiet here and I spent every morning walking on the beach. Still asking God for answers to my many questions about my purpose in life, His will, etc., He answered in a very clear voice. He answered me with a simple, "Harriet, love me." Over and over I heard His message. I couldn't believe this. Is this all He wants from me? I already love Him. Why did He not want more from me?

My understanding changed. Before, I was searching for an immediate answer and one that would spotlight me. This was not at all what God had in mind. When I decided to trust Him, my relationship with God did change. I have learned that loving God is a process that is not complete overnight. Loving God is not simple. Loving God has meant studying his Word, spending time in prayer and listening. This relationship has healed, filled me with an inner joy and made me more complete. I love my God as a king, a father, a friend. He is truly the love of my life!

I Peter 1:8 says, "You love Him even though you have never seen Him, though not seeing Him, you trust Him, and even now you are happy with the inexpressible joy that comes from Heaven itself."

Dear Heavenly Father,

Thank You for revealing yourself to me. Through the process of knowing and loving You, I have received such joy. Help me as I continue in this walk. My desire is to please You and honor You and to be Your servant. In Your precious Son's name. Amen

*Harriet Woodson*

# A PRAYER FOR MY MOTHER

*D*ear Heavenly Father,
On this beautiful day, here in Atlanta with windows opened and a light summer breeze blowing, I've been sitting and thinking what could I give my mother for her birthday. Seventy-four years old on June 9, I know my mother doesn't want or need anything materialistic. Frankly, the best gift I could give her is to jump on a jet plane, fly to Chicago, and give her a big hug and tell her how much I love her.

I will be doing that later this summer, so maybe this is the perfect time to offer You a prayer in thanksgiving and gratitude for my mom, and at the same time let her know.

Lord, as I reflect on my blessings, my parents are truly one of them. Through Your divine will and purpose, they have raised, guided, supported and instilled in their six children strong Christian values—love and respect for one another, fairness, and compassion. As a child of theirs and Yours, I am grateful. As a parent myself, I pray that I, too, may follow their lead, and impart the same wisdom and love that my parents have for me to my children. How fortunate we are to be able to reflect upon Your Son's life on this earth as a guide for us all. May all that we do bring You honor and glory.

Lord, I pray that as my mother has experienced challenges and hardships in her life, that I also have the grace, strength, courage and faith in You that she has exhibited all her life. Early on, my mother introduced me to her spiritual values. At a young age, we said evening prayers together, a very warm and vivid memory which even includes her mother, my grandmother. She sent me to catechism, later Sacred Heart, but always her daily patience, understanding and tolerance set an invisible but powerful tone.

Lord, I pray that the gift of encouragement that my mother gives so freely remains a quality that I give to my children, spouse, siblings and friends. I pray to be a "balcony" person, like my mother, be uplifting as well as uplift all concerns to You.

Lord, most of all, I pray that the Holy Spirit will descend upon my family, friends and even my enemies, and that we may be filled with the desire to know and to love and to serve You; and that we may benefit from the fruits of the Spirit—joy, peace, love, patience, kindness, goodness, faithfulness, gentleness, and self-control.

Lord, I pray that we may all trust in You with all our hearts, and know that You are in control of all things in our lives. I pray that any anger we have in our hearts is given over to You and we forgive those who have hurt us, so we may be free to do Your will, love one another as You love us. I know that You often work silently in our lives. Sometimes I wish You made a little more noise, but I know You have our best interests at heart.

Lord, I honor my mother, which honors You. Thank You for her and for loving her. You showed her Your unconditional love, and she in turn shows us. May all the angels in Heaven wrap their beautiful wings around her, my dad, my brothers and sisters and my children, to light, to guard and rule and guide us all for years to come, so we may celebrate many more birthdays. Amen

*Story Evans*

## ABIDING IN HIS LOVE

*H*eavenly Father,
I cannot begin to fathom the depth of Your patience with me. Here I am again wondering how I could wander so far from Your presence. I know in reality that You have not pulled away from me—You promise in Your Word to never leave me or forsake me. But still, the distance I feel—the lack of deep intimacy with You—is here again. When I reach this place— as I must have a zillion times—You faithfully lead me back to John 15. You speak to me, so clearly in Your Word that I can almost hear Your voice! And for the zillionth time You say softly, "I am the vine, You are the branches...Abide in me and I will abide in you. No branch can bear fruit by itself, it must remain in the vine. Abide in my love." Lord, the idea of a branch trying to bear fruit on its own efforts is absurd. And so it is with me! Thank you that all You ask of me is to abide in You, to remain in You, to stay in You, to dwell in You and allow You to love me. It is only then that I can experience that intimate union with You and be open and available for You to use me for Your kingdom.

*Julia Izlar*

## *MY BEST FRIEND*

*I* am at the end of one painful, yet growing and loving year. You have shown me Your Face so often, but at times I have missed Your Smile. Please dear God, open my eyes hourly to walk with You, and hold my hand without letting me go.

Our move from Atlanta has placed me away from special friends and loved ones, but has challenged me to love You as my best friend. It's been very lonely. I've needed someone to share the loneliness with, to encourage me with my children, to walk me through surgery, to find a home for my family, to help my children develop and build friends, and to support my husband. No one was there.

This year has been hard, and I have really had to stretch...But you are faithful Lord, and I must count my blessings—a kind and loving husband of sixteen years; three awesome ten-year-old boys who are so full of life and fun, a joy for me and a challenge to raise as Godly men; a five year old who "hung the Moon" with his sweet and gentle spirit whom I adore; and then the blessing and surprise of all, at age forty, a new baby girl who rules the roost! Lord, your blessings are endless.

Help me count them hourly. Your gifts are good, your love unending—but Lord, your desire to have all of me is evident.

I ask, God, for you to give me your character and teach me the patience to wait on you. You have a perfect plan for my life—give me the courage to see it one day at a time.

Thank you, Lord, for hearing my prayer.

*Lynn Pitts*

## *FRIENDSHIP*

*O*ne of the ways I feel touched by God is through the people He places in my life—the ones He places there to inspire me and encourage me; the ones He places there to nurture and to love me; the ones He lovingly places in my life to bring me closer to Him. These are lives that reflect his teachings and His great commandment to "love they neighbor as thyself."

As God so lovingly places these people in my life, He in turn calls me to live a life that reflects this commandment so they too will be drawn closer to Him.

A dear friend recently told me how much she admired my selflessness and my "seeming" ability to put so many others before me. While certainly a gracious compliment, it is only with God's continued guidance that any of us can live this way. I am reminded daily of His beautiful scripture in Matthew 5:16, "Let your light so shine before men, that they may see your good works and give glory to your Father who is in Heaven."

*Lora Smith*

# HIS BEAUTIFUL PRESENCE IS IN EACH OF US

*W*hen I was pregnant with my son, and then after his birth, I became increasingly aware of the preciousness of so many moments. Even ordinary conversations and situations took on new meaning and significance. Clothed in all his innocence, this uncomplicated, perfect, clean little spirit just seemed to have a way of bringing God's Presence into so many situations. Even the edges of a bad day or a bad attitude could shift. I was reminded how, in sharp contrast, we as adults have allowed the world and ourselves to strip us of His beautiful innocence. We have instead clothed ourselves with so many different masks—our pride, our vanity, our greed, our jealousies—all of these preventing us from being the very people God intended us to be.

Within each of us is your beautiful Presence that can only be illuminated and reflected when we strip away these layers of self.

Dear Lord, teach us to strip away these layers of pride, will, greed, vanity and self so that Your Light will shine and that we can be who we are called to be for each other. Amen

*Robin Willis*

# I LOVE YOU, LORD

*D*ear Heavenly Father,
I love You so much! You are so incredibly awesome. Thank You so much for Your unconditional love. How can You possibly want to give me as much as you do when I have nothing more than my soul to offer. You died for me, Lord—that is more than I could ever ask for. Even when I am not faithful, You stay with me always. You never turn you back on me. A wonderful example of that comes from something one of my Christian youth leaders taught me. He talked about the "Roman Handshake." This handshake is very different from the traditional one. In a Roman Handshake, you grab on to each other's forearm. This way, if one person lets go, the other is still holding on so that person can grab on again. Glen used this analogy to describe our relationship with Jesus Christ: We can let go but Jesus will hold on forever.

Lord Jesus, I thank You so very much for never letting go of me. Your grace to forgive us is truly amazing. Sending your Son to die for us was the most kind, loving, unselfish and thoughtful act that has ever been preformed. I am so grateful for that, and I praise Your name.

Please help me to live up to my responsibilities and

duties of being a good and faithful Christian. Please grant me the patience and understanding to go throughout the day knowing and trusting that Your will for me is good.

I thank you for each day you have blessed me with and for all the many gifts you have given me.

I pray that I can become a much better Christian and love You more and more. You are the only, one, true God. You are something so incredible, not even words can describe You. Your everlasting love is so wonderful. Lord, I take so much for granted. Each little thing you give me is such a blessing and I should be so much more thankful. I need to learn not to complain about things I don't have, but be thankful for what I do have.

Please help me to follow more in Your footsteps and act in Your holiness, doing things with love and kindness. You are so good to me and I thank You for that. I love You with all my heart. Please take my hand and guide me on your path to Heaven. Help me to follow in Your Holiness and lead me to righteousness. I love you so much.

*Emmy Hewlett*
*Age 14*
*Daughter of Cindy Hewlett*

# DAY BY DAY COUNT YOUR BLESSINGS

Day by day Your blessings fall
upon us in every way.
But we never seem to take the time or
way to say
How very thankful we are to You.

The muscles we use to walk up and
down the stairs,
or the arms we used to comb our hair.
The breezes when days are hot,
The smiles we receive whether we
like them or not.

For the rain and the flowers
and the food we devour.
The hugs and kisses we apprehend
from our family and friends.

Most importantly, we give thanks to You,
who gave His only Son to cleanse our
guilt through and through.
From all the evil desires

that will burn us in the fires.
We long to be like Him in each and every way
so that we can grow closer to You every day.
Amen

*Mary Stuart Young*
*Age 14*
*Daughter of Studie Young*

## AN EASTER PRAYER

Just risen today
Excellent teacher
Such a kind person
Unusual man
Serves the Lord

Great Creator
Oh, so holy
Does great things

*Abby Evans*
*Age 10*
*Daughter of Story Evans*

# "CALLED" TO TOUCH OTHERS

*I* used to think that the only people who were "called" to serve God were missionaries and ministers...oh, and nuns, of course. However, God made it quite clear to me that that was not the case when He touched my life almost twelve years ago.

It was shortly after the birth of my second child that one evening I heard a minister on TV ask, "Is Christ the center of your life?" I knew He wasn't, and as I sat looking into the eyes of my latest blessing, I realized I had to change. After I put my little one to sleep and turned off the TV, I sat and began to pray. There was no blinding light, no angelic appearances, no burning bush...just a simple tear that followed a simple prayer, "Lord, I know that I have been the center of my life, and yet you have blessed me anyway. I pray for forgiveness, a desire to know You better, and I pray, Lord, that You might use my life to make a difference for You."

The next few days and weeks I knew I had been forgiven and God had, in fact, given me a desire to know Him. I bought new Bibles and spent time in prayer, enrolled in classes and made new Christian friends, all of whom helped me to understand God better.

After a few years of seeking God, I began to feel God seeking me. My church asked me to teach a group of twelve women the Bible. "Me?" I thought, "I'm not sure I can do this. I must spend time in prayer. This can't be right. I just had my fourth child. Surely God wants me to simply be at home for my children and my husband." I wanted to be a great wife and mother.

I decided to write a letter to Billy Graham's wife, hoping she could give me some guidance here. While she was out of the country, I received a long typed letter and several books from the head of the organization. Let me share some excerpts from the letter.

"The best news is that you are a child of God and that He has trusted you with four beautiful children…believing that you will do everything possible to implant in their lives the Word of God. WE also commend you for seeking the opportunity to share the Good News of the Bible. Isaiah 55:11 says, "God will bless his Word wherever it goes and it will bear fruit." He wants you to share the Bible WHEREVER you have the opportunity. You also indicated that you are anxious about this and do not feel worthy. You are only an instrument being used by the Holy Spirit. He will lead you as you are preparing your lessons. Remember, 'I can do all things through Christ who strengthens me,' (Phil 4:13) and, 'Ye have not chosen me but I have chosen you.' (John 15:16)"

After this letter and the encouragement of my husband, I decided I would give it a try. After all, it was only one morning a week for a year. Well, I must confess that I cried my eyes out the night before my first lesson because I was so fearful of blowing it for God.

God had to show me that I could not do this on my own. He had to do it for me. I had to give up on my ability and trust in His.

Well, guess what? You can't out give God. Today (twelve years later), my family has been continually blessed as my children and my husband have come to know the Lord and as we meet weekly to study His Word. Before, I was concerned that the Bible study would take away from my role in the family, only to realize that it is dependence on God's guidance that makes us better wives and mothers. And what happened to the Bible study? Well...

Today, forever humbled by the grace and power of God, I stand in a chapel looking upon 250 sweet faces, and a witness to the many lives He continues to change. Just as God has touched me and my family in such a powerful way, He has also touched the many lives from our Bible study represented in this book. God continues to call each of us to touch others for his name sake.

Dear Heavenly Father,

How can I ever thank You for what you have done in my life? I pray, Lord, that you will continue to use me, my husband and my children to reach out to others. May we always remember that "we can do all things through Christ who strengthens us." In his precious name, Amen.

*Nancy McGuirk*

# LETTER FROM MARCIA HILL

*D*ear Friends,
Some of you may wonder why I have such love
and faith in God. I believe that God does perform
miracles in both small and great ways. I am not angry
with God for not healing me of cancer. I am sad that His
will for me has not taken that path yet, but He has given
me so many daily blessings. I am grateful for the gift of
today and I wake up with a prayer of thanks. I feel so
blessed to be experiencing each moment of life. It fills
me with a sense of wonderment, joy and contentment
and I go to bed each night with prayers of gratitude for
the opportunities of today and the promise of tomorrow.

I believe the prayer of faith comes from walking
with God through each day. I am here today because
God has taken my life and embraced it with his protec-
tive love. There is never a moment of the day when, if I
quiet myself, I do not feel God's presence. In my darkest
moments when I have lost my courage and strength He
has come to me with his radiating strength, held me and
pushed me forward, back into life. God has held me
close with His embracing love. He has walked hand and
hand with me. At other times when physically I was too

weak to go one more step, He carried me up one mountain after another. He has always promised me a magnificent view from the top and I have experienced that beauty many times, as well as the exhilaration of success at being there time and time again. God never promised me an easy road but He promised He would always be there and I have opened my heart to Him and He has never let me down. I have learned that life for all of us is filled with bumpy roads. He did not say he would take the pain or hurt away but that we can trust Him to take care of us. If you open yourself in prayer to Him, He will walk you through whatever life has put in front of you.

I walk in prayer with God throughout the day—that is how I have survived. I am proud of that. It is no secret, but something I want you to understand. I have learned the gift of love that comes from being gentle with yourself and learning to forgive hurtful relationships or things from the past. I have grown in my personal relationship with God to understand I am worthy of his unconditional love. I have felt the incredible sense of peace that comes from surrendering to

God's love and letting Him shelter you with His grace.

Prayer is my way of connecting intimately with God. I am learning to expand my world of prayer to reach out to address the needs of others. I deeply desire for my prayers to touch and positively change the lives of others. I pray that we remember to stay centered with God and that He will use our relationship with Him to make a positive difference in the lives of every person we touch. Let us always remember life is lived moment by moment. We are only sure of this moment, so let us embrace the gift of life God has given us with a positive attitude. The way we approach life does make a difference.

*Marcia Hill*
*April 10, 1995*